Food and Festivals

BRAZIL

Mariana Serra

RSVP
RAINTREE
STECK-VAUGHN
PUBLISHERS
A Steck-Vaughn Company

Austin, Texas

Food and Festivals
BRAZIL

Other titles:

Brazil ● The Caribbean ● China ● France ● Germany
India ● Israel ● Italy ● Kenya ● Mexico ● West Africa

Cover photograph: A boy carries home a basket of vegetables from the market.

Title page: A boy dressed as one of the Candomblé gods

Contents page: A dancer in colorful costume taking part in the June Festivals

Published by Raintree Steck-Vaughn Publishers, an imprint of Steck-Vaughn Company

Printed in Italy. Bound in the United States.
1 2 3 4 5 6 7 8 9 0 03 02 01 00 99

Library of Congress Cataloging-in-Publication Data
Serra, Mariana.
Brazil / Mariana Serra.
    p.   cm.—(Food and festivals)
Includes bibliographical references and index.
Summary: Discusses some of the foods enjoyed in Brazil and describes special foods that are part of such specific celebrations as Carnaval and the Bambá Bull festival. Includes recipes.
ISBN 0-7398-1406-0 (hard)
0-7398-0960-1 (soft)
1. Cookery, Brazilian—Juvenile literature.
2. Food habits—Brazil—Juvenile literature.
3. Festivals—Brazil—Juvenile literature.
4. Brazil—Social life and customs—Juvenile literature.
[1. Cookery, Brazilian. 2. Food habits—Brazil.
3. Festivals—Brazil. 4. Holidays—Brazil. 5. Brazil—Social life and customs]
I. Title. II. Series.
TX716.B6S47 2000
394.1'0981—dc21   99-13473

CONTENTS

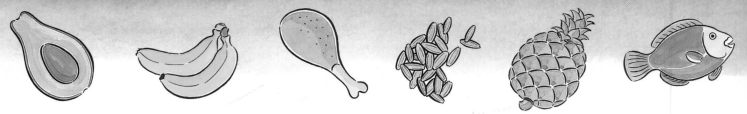

Brazil and Its Food

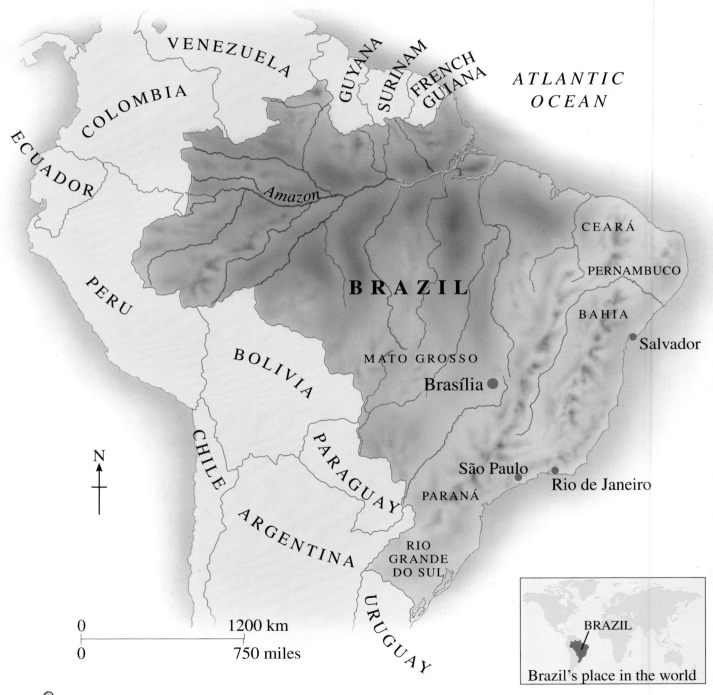

VENEZUELA

GUYANA

SURINAM

FRENCH GUIANA

ATLANTIC OCEAN

COLOMBIA

ECUADOR

Amazon

CEARÁ

PERNAMBUCO

PERU

BAHIA

Salvador

BRAZIL

MATO GROSSO

Brasília

BOLIVIA

N

CHILE

PARAGUAY

São Paulo

Rio de Janeiro

PARANÁ

ARGENTINA

RIO GRANDE DO SUL

URUGUAY

0   1200 km

0   750 miles

BRAZIL

Brazil's place in the world

4

BLACK BEANS AND RICE

Brazilians eat black beans and rice almost every day. These foods are very nutritious. *Feijoada* (pronounced fay-joo-ada) is a dish made with black beans.

FISH

Most Brazilians live near rivers or the coast, where they can find a delicious variety of seafood and fish. Dishes such as the mimini fish shown here are popular.

CASSAVA

Cassava is a staple food in the rain forest in the north. You can see some on sale at the bottom of this picture. Throughout Brazil, cassava is used in many sweet and savory dishes.

SUGAR AND OIL

Sugarcane is grown on plantations like the one in this picture. Oil for cooking is taken from palm trees. Sugar and oil are the main energy foods for people living in the dry northeast.

CATTLE, PIGS, AND CHICKENS

Cattle, pigs, and chickens are kept on big farms. Brazilians eat lots of meat, and barbecued meat is very popular.

FRUIT

Many exotic types of fruit, such as graviola and açaí, grow in the wild. Oranges, bananas, and other fruits are grown on large plantations.

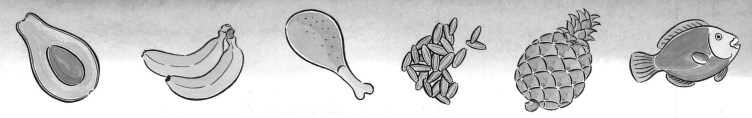

Food and Farming

Brazil is one of the largest countries in the world. It covers more than half the continent of South America. More than 165 million people live there.

In the north of Brazil lies the world's biggest rain forest, called the Amazon. The climate here is hot and wet. Northeastern Brazil is always hot and dry, almost like a desert. In Rio Grande do Sul, in the south, winters can be so cold that it sometimes snows.

▼ A farm worker with his children on a sugarcane plantation in Pernambuco

Rice and black beans

There are so many different climates in Brazil that a wide variety of crops can be grown there. Rice and black beans are the two staple foods. Black beans are grown anywhere where the weather is hot enough (except in the rain forest). Rice needs warm weather and wet soil, so it is grown in the swampy fields in western Brazil.

▲ These people in São Paulo are helping themselves to some *feijoada,* which is a favorite dish made with black beans.

◄ Farmers harvesting rice in western Brazil

7

▲This market stall in Ceará sells cassava (lower right) along with other fruits and vegetables.

Growing crops

Most fruits and vegetables come from very large plantations. These are found all over Brazil except in the rain forest. It is difficult to grow crops in the rain forest. Rain forest peoples move from place to place, gathering plants that grow in the wild for food.

◀ A cowboy rounds up a herd of cattle in Mato Grosso.

▼ This man in Paraná is preparing *churrasco*.

Barbecues

Farmers in the west keep thousands of cattle on vast ranches. The huge herds have to be moved regularly to fresh grazing land.

Most Brazilians are great meat lovers. The cowboys of the south, who are called gaúchos (pronounced gow-chos), say that they make the best barbecues in the world. They cover the large joints of meat in rock salt before they cook them, and the cooked meat is called *churrasco* (pronounced shur-hass-co).

◀ This girl is cooking turtles, traditional food among the peoples of the rain forest.

People and religions

The peoples of the rain forest were the first to live in Brazil. Some of their descendants still speak their traditional languages, and they have their own religious beliefs, too. But most Brazilians today are Catholics, and their language is Portuguese. That is because, in 1500, settlers from Portugal arrived in Brazil and ruled the country for more than 300 years.

The Portuguese settlers brought slaves from Africa to work on their plantations. The slaves had their own religious beliefs. As time passed, these beliefs became a faith called Candomblé.

Candomblé followers believe in many gods, who are called *orixás*. In Brazil, it is normal to belong to more than one religion at the same time. Many Candomblé followers believe that their gods are the same as the Catholic saints, and most Catholics like to join in the non-Christian festivals.

This woman belongs ▶ to the Candomblé faith. She is selling traditional food from Bahia.

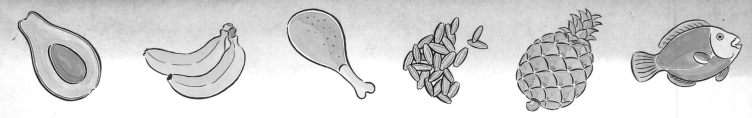

Carnaval

Carnival in Brazil is called *Carnaval*, and some people describe it as the biggest party in the world. Carnival began in Europe, hundreds of years ago. It was originally celebrated by Catholics. In Brazil today, it is enjoyed by people of all religions. Some of the most spectacular celebrations are held in Rio de Janeiro.

▼Children dressed up for *Carnaval* in Salvador

Samba school parades

▲ A glittering *Carnaval* parade in Rio de Janeiro

At *Carnaval* time the streets of Rio are filled with people dancing to the sound of the samba. Samba is a type of Brazilian music that uses drums to create a strong rhythm. It developed from the African music used in Candomblé ceremonies. During *Carnaval*, different samba schools hold colorful street parades. These last for four days (and nights!).

SAMBA SCHOOLS

Community groups known as samba schools spend all year preparing stunning costumes and dances for the official *Carnaval* parades. They compete against each other to see who can create the best costumes and music.

How *Carnaval* began

In the Middle Ages, Christians in Europe celebrated carnival in the days before Lent began. Lent is a period when it is traditional for Christians to go without meat, or even without any food at all. It is a way to remember the last days in the life of Jesus. Carnival was a time to eat a lot, drink a lot, and have a lot of fun before the fasting began. The Portuguese brought the carnival tradition to Brazil.

▲ These delicious fruits have been prepared for a *Carnaval* banquet.

ROYAL FOR A DAY

In the old European carnivals, kings, queens, lords, and ladies would dress up as poor people to join in the festival. Their servants chose their own carnival kings and became royal for a day. In Brazil, African slaves were allowed a few days to party and make fun of their masters by dressing up as them.

Everywhere in Brazil, ▶ people take to the streets to dance and have fun during *Carnaval*.

The flavor of *Carnaval*

▲ Hot chilies add a spicy flavor to pepper-scented rice.

Most Brazilians no longer fast during Lent, but they still like to prepare special meals to celebrate *Carnaval*. Pepper-scented rice is a *Carnaval* favorite. It shows how the different cooking styles of the peoples who have come to live in Brazil have mingled together. Rice is popular in Portuguese cooking, and the spicy peppers show the African taste for hot foods.

Pepper-scented Rice

EQUIPMENT

Chopping board
Sharp knife
Measuring cup
Teakettle

Tablespoon
Large saucepan
Wooden spoon

INGREDIENTS (for 2–3)

1 Tablespoon of vegetable oil
1 Small onion, diced fine
1 Garlic clove, minced
1 Cup Long-grain rice
1 Chili pepper
2 Cups of hot water
$\frac{1}{2}$ Teaspoon of salt

1 Pour the vegetable oil into the saucepan and heat it for a few seconds.

2 Add the onion, garlic, and rice, and fry gently, stirring for about 4 minutes.

3 Add the chili pepper, hot water, and salt. Stir well and bring to a boil.

4 Simmer for 15–20 minutes. When the rice is quite soft and the water has gone, remove the pepper and serve.

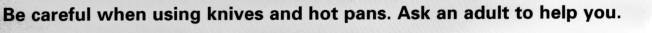

Be careful when using knives and hot pans. Ask an adult to help you.

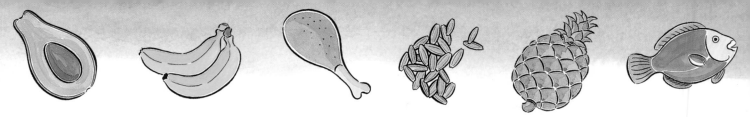

Bumbá Bull

The Bumbá Bull festival, or *Boi Bumbá,* is celebrated in many villages throughout the Amazon area. The celebrations are linked to an ancient rain forest legend. Some people travel long distances to celebrate the festival in the small village of Paratins. The journey by boat can last up to a week. In the village, they dress up in colorful costumes, and there is music, dancing, and fireworks.

▼ A rain forest family in their village home near the Amazon River.

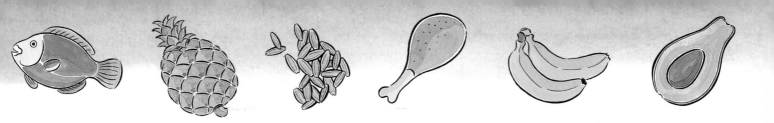

The legend of the Bumbá bull

The legend of the Bumbá bull tells of a pregnant woman who was having cravings for certain types of food. One day, her cravings got so bad that she asked her husband to kill his boss's prized bull.

When her husband's boss found out, he was very unhappy. He called the local *pajé*, who is the religious leader of the rain forest people. The *pajé* danced around the dead bull, casting spells. After much effort, he was able to bring the bull back to life, making everyone dance for joy.

These people are ▶ dressed up as the characters in the Bumbá bull legend.

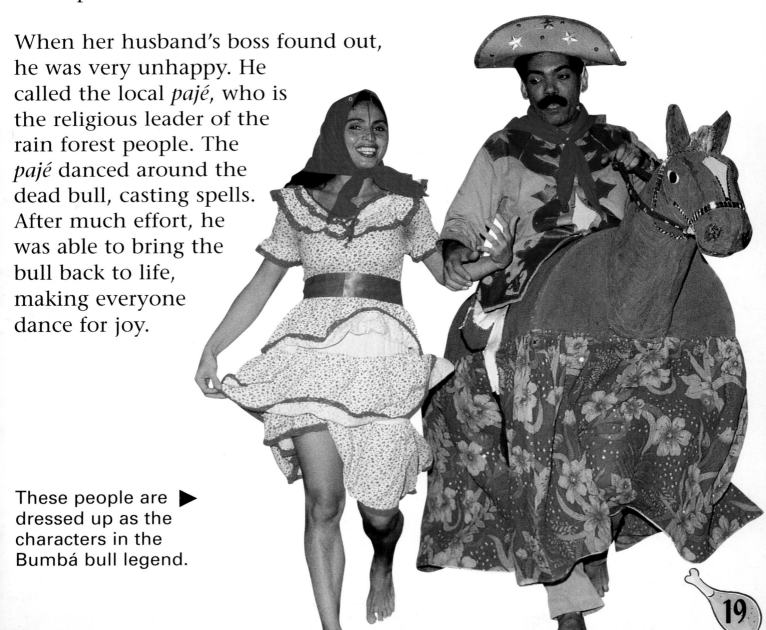

19

FISHING IN THE AMAZON

The traditional way for rain forest people to catch their fish is by standing in the river and catching the fish on a spear. This can be dangerous if piranhas come their way. Piranhas are fish with big teeth that can attack swimmers.

Festival food

Because the man in the rain forest legend liked his bull so much, people avoid eating meat during the Bumbá Bull festival. Sometimes they have fish, which they catch in the Amazon River. There is a recipe for a fish dish on the opposite page. This recipe also uses coconut milk, which is a very popular ingredient in Brazilian cookery.

▼ Fish dishes such as mimini fish are very popular in Brazil.

Mimini fish

EQUIPMENT

Chopping board   Spatula
Sharp knife   Wooden spoon
Garlic press   Plate
Frying pan

INGREDIENTS (for 1)

1/4 lb. (100 g) White fish, such as cod
1 Tablespooon of vegetable oil
1 Medium onion, chopped
1 Clove of garlic, crushed
3 Tomatoes, chopped
Salt and pepper
14 oz. (400 ml) Can of coconut milk
1 Serving of cooked rice

Heat the oil in a large frying pan for a few seconds, add the fish and fry until golden. Put it on a plate and set it aside.

Fry the onions and garlic until soft.

Stir in the tomatoes and simmer them for 3 minutes. Add a little salt and pepper.

Put the fried fish back in the pan and stir in the coconut milk. Bring the mixture to a boil. Serve immediately with rice.

Be careful when using knives and hot pans. Ask an adult to help you.

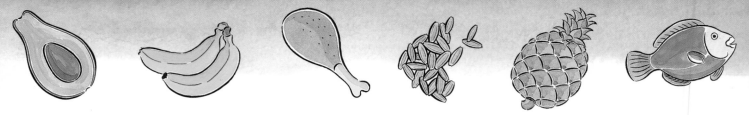

June Festivals

Catholic traditions are very important in Brazil. The June Festivals, or *Festas Juninas*, are held in honor of Saint Anthony, Saint Peter, and Saint John. Saint John has the greatest number of followers, and all of them look forward to Saint John's Day, especially the children.

In parts of northeast Brazil, people believe that Saint John protects the harvest of corn and green beans, so they will all have plenty of food in the year ahead. Saint John's festival is celebrated when these crops are harvested.

▼ Harvesting corn in eastern Brazil

Saint John's Day

Brazilian Catholics begin the holy day of Saint John by going to church for a special mass. At school, children listen to stories about the saint.

In the afternoon, outdoor parties begin. Everyone dresses up in the traditional clothes worn by the farm workers of central Brazil. People play traditional games, such as jumping over a bonfire or trying to climb up a slippery stick. It is a day of fun for everyone.

A dancer in traditional ▶ clothes at a Saint John's Day party.

23

At all the June Festivals, Brazilians like to eat food made from corn, the crop protected by Saint John. They use corn to make puddings and cakes, as well as eating it on the cob. You can find out how to make a delicious corn cake on the opposite page.

▲ Corn cake is a traditional Saint John's Day dish.

MUSIC FOR ALL

People enjoy listening and dancing to *forró* music at Saint John's Day parties. *Forró* music is played on accordions and percussion instruments. The word *Forró* comes from the time when the British came to Brazil to build the first railroads. Every month, the British bosses invited the builders to a party that was open for all. "For all" became *Forró*.

◀ A young girl enjoys corn on the cob.

Corn Cake

EQUIPMENT

Can opener

Food processor
or bowl and whisk

Wooden spoon
or spatula

Large greased
loaf pan

Oven mitts

Wire rack

INGREDIENTS

11 oz. (325 g) Can of corn, drained

7 Tablespoons Butter, softened

1 Scant cup Wholewheat flour

3 Eggs, beaten

14 oz. (400 ml) Can of coconut milk

1 Tablespoon of baking powder

2 Cups granulated sugar

Set the oven to 350° F (180°C). Put all the ingredients into a food processor or bowl and blend or mix until smooth.

Pour the mixture into the loaf pan.

Bake for approximately 50 minutes. To test if the cake is done, stick a toothpick into the center—it should come out clean.

Turn the cake onto a wire rack to cool, then slice and serve.

Be careful when using the oven. Ask an adult to help you.

Bonfim

Salvador is the oldest city in Brazil, and the people who live there have kept the Candomblé religion alive. Festivals held in honor of the different gods, called *orixás,* are celebrated in Salvador throughout the year.

▼ Candomblé women in Bahia dress in white to honor the god Oxalá.

The *Bonfim* festival in January honors the god Oxalá, father of all *orixás*. Many Brazilians say that Oxalá is the same as Jesus Christ. White roses are Oxalá's favorite flowers, and black beans are his favorite food.

THE *ORIXAS*

Oxalá is linked with Jesus Christ, and the other *orixás* are linked with Christian saints. Each *orixá* has a favorite food, too.

Orixá	Christian saint	Favorite food
Ogum	St. Anthony	Yam
Oxóssi	St. George	Corn with coconut
Oxumaré	St. Bartholomew	Beans with corn and palm oil.

Candomblé followers dress in white for the *Bonfim* festival, as a symbol of peace and purity.

Thousands of people join in a procession to the Church of Our Lord Jesus of *Bonfim*. There, they watch some of the Candomblé women wash the steps outside the church with rose water.

Later, people have fun dancing to traditional Candomblé music for many hours.

These Bahia women ▶ are taking part in the ceremony of washing the church steps, like the ceremony that takes place at *Bonfim*.

▲ These colorful *Bonfim* ribbons are believed to be lucky.

Oxalá's market

Near the *Bonfim* church, Candomblé women called *Bahianas* set up market stands. The traditional goods on sale include *Bonfim* lucky ribbons and the black bean soup that is Oxalá's favorite food. There is a recipe for black bean soup on the opposite page.

▼ Black beans are used in a variety of dishes, like this delicious soup.

Black Bean Soup

EQUIPMENT

Chopping board   Can opener
Sharp knife   Ladle
Saucepan   Food processor

This recipe can also be made without a food processor—see Step 3.

INGREDIENTS (for 2–3)

8 oz. (250 g) black beans, or dried kidney beans, soaked overnight
1 Onion, chopped
1 Garlic clove, chopped
1 14.5 oz. (410 g) Can of chopped tomatoes
1 Bouillon cube, any flavor
1 Tablespoon of chopped parsley
1 Tablespoon of chopped coriander
Crisp bacon as garnish

Drain the soaked beans. Put them in a saucepan. Cover them with cold water, and bring them to a boil. Boil them for ten minutes, partially covered.

Crumble the bouillon cube into the pan and add the other ingredients. Cover and simmer for 15–20 minutes. Add more water if necessary.

Ladle the mixture into a food processor and blend until smooth, or simmer for another 10 minutes.

Pour the soup back into the pan and reheat. Serve with crisp bacon sprinkled on the top.

Be careful when using hot pans and knives. Ask an adult to help you.

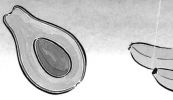

Glossary

Accordions Instruments that are played by squeezing an air bag in and out and pressing keys on a keyboard.

Catholics Christians who are led by the Pope in Rome, Italy.

Climate The type of weather that an area usually has.

Cravings Very strong feelings of needing something, such as a certain type of food.

Descendants Relatives of people who died a long time ago.

Fast To go without food or without certain foods.

Mass An important Catholic ceremony.

Nutritious Full of nutrients, the parts of foods that help our bodies grow and stay healthy.

Plantations Large farms where crops are grown usually so that they can be sold to other countries.

Rain forest Thick forest that grows in areas where the climate is hot and wet.

Ranches Large farms where animals, especially cattle, are raised.

Settlers People who have traveled from one country to live in another country.

Slaves People who are owned by other people. They are not paid for their work and have no freedom.

Staple foods Foods that are the main part of people's everyday diet.

Swampy Wet. A swamp is an area of very wet land, sometimes thickly covered with plants.

Picture acknowledgments
Chapel Studios/Zul Mukhida 5 (top right), 16, 20, 24 (top), 28 (bottom); Sue Cunningham *Cover*, Title page, contents page, 9 (bottom), 12, 13, 14, 18, 19, 23, 24 (bottom), 27, 28 (top); Eye Ubiquitous/James Davis 11; Hutchison 26; Impact 22/Marco Siqueira; Panos 7 (bottom)/Sean Sprague; Edward Parker 5 (center right), 5 (bottom left), 6, 9 (top), 10; South American Pictures 5 (top left)/Jason P. Howe, 5 (center left)/Tony Morrison, 7 (top)/Jason P. Howe, 8/Tony Morrison, 15/Tony Morrison; Wayland Picture Library/Julia Waterlow 5 (bottom right).

Fruit and vegetable artwork is by Tina Barber. The map on page 4 is by Peter Bull and Hardlines. The step-by-step artwork is by Judy Stevens.

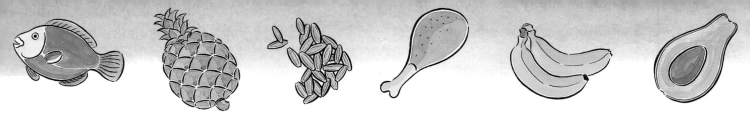

Books to Read

Bender, Evelyn. *Brazil* (Let's Visit Places and Peoples of the World). New York: Chelsea House, 1990.

Carpenter, Mark. *Brazil: An Awakening Giant*. New York: Dillon, 1988.

Lewington Anna. *Rain Forest Amerindians* (Threatened Cultures). Austin, TX: Raintree Steck-Vaughn, 1992.

Lewington, Anna and Edward Parker. *Brazil* (Economically Developing Countries). Austin, TX: Thomson Learning, 1995.

Morrison, Marion. *The Amazon Rain Forest and Its People* (People and Places). Austin, TX: Thomson Learning, 1993.

————. *Brazil* (Country Fact Files). Austin, TX: Raintree Steck-Vaughn, 1993.

————. *Brazil* (Country Insights). Austin, TX: Raintree Steck-Vaughn, 1997.

Index

Page numbers in **bold** mean there is a photograph on the page.